The Empire

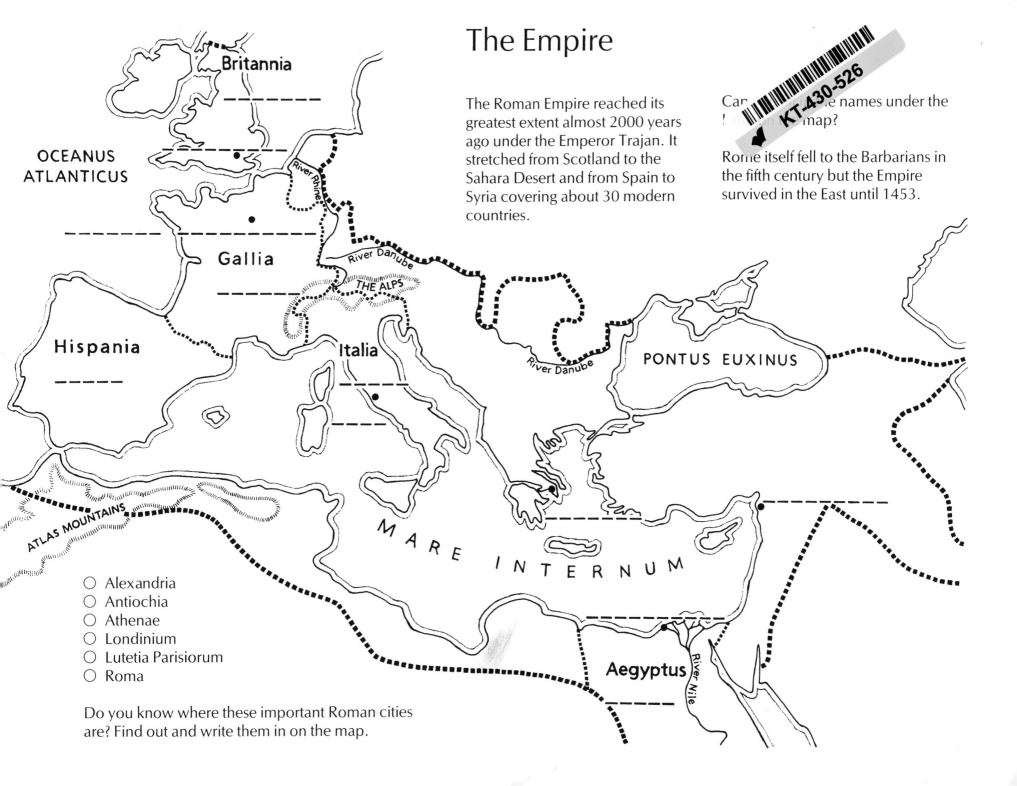

Britannia

OCEANUS
ATLANTICUS

The Roman Empire reached its greatest extent almost 2000 years ago under the Emperor Trajan. It stretched from Scotland to the Sahara Desert and from Spain to Syria covering about 30 modern countries.

Ca_____ _____ names under the _____ ___ map?

Rome itself fell to the Barbarians in the fifth century but the Empire survived in the East until 1453.

Gallia

River Rhine

River Danube

THE ALPS

River Danube

PONTUS EUXINUS

Hispania

Italia

ATLAS MOUNTAINS

M A R E   I N T E R N U M

○ Alexandria
○ Antiochia
○ Athenae
○ Londinium
○ Lutetia Parisiorum
○ Roma

Aegyptus

River Nile

Do you know where these important Roman cities are? Find out and write them in on the map.

The Emperors

Rome had many emperors. They were often good leaders, but some are famous for other reasons as well. See if you can work out which drawing goes with which Emperor. (answers on p.16)

Nero (AD54–68) was awarded first prize in the singing contest at the Olympic Games, even though he was said to have 'a voice worse than a crow'.

3

4

Hadrian (AD117–38) had many different interests. He was described as 'eager for travel, . . . to see with his own eyes everything which he had read about the places of the earth'.

2

Trajan (AD98–117) was a popular commander and when on campaign is said to have lived like the ordinary soldiers 'and cheerfully ate his rations in the open with them'.

Marcus Aurelius (AD161–80) is remembered for the books he wrote on philosophy. He was a firm but fair ruler who was said to have 'made the bad good and the good very good'.

1

Rome

The city of Rome was the heart of the Empire, and at the heart of the city was the Forum, which had many great and beautiful buildings, such as temples and markets. The senate met there too. Senators were wealthy Roman nobles who helped the Emperor to govern the people and the Empire.

Caius Flavius Priscus is a senator. His friends call him Gaius. Here he is talking to some friends in the Forum. They are deciding what to do today. They could go to the Colosseum to see the gladiators fighting (look at the front cover). Or perhaps they could go to watch chariot races at the circus. (On the back cover, there is a chariot racing game to play.)

Look at pictures A and B. They are supposed to be the same but picture B has 8 mistakes in it. Can you spot them and finish the drawing? Watch out particularly for columns and statues.

A

B

3

In the country . . .

Many familiar things had not been invented in Roman times. This picture of Gaius' house *(villa)* and farm shows 8 things which the Romans did not have. Can you find them? (answers on p.16)

Voyage by sea

The emperor has given Gaius command of a legion in Britain. He travels by sea from Rome to Gaul and marches north before crossing the Channel to Britain.

What sort of ship does he use? Join the dots to finish the picture.

In Britain

This map shows some of the main Roman sites in Britain. You can visit them all. The drawings illustrate five of them.

Can you guess which they are from the clues? (answers are on p.16)

Constantine was declared Emperor by the army in this northern city.

1 — — — —

The hot springs of the goddess Sulis-Minerva were the main attraction of this Roman spa town.

2 — — — —

Near Chichester, this fine villa is believed to have been the palace of Cogidubnus, a British chieftain who befriended the Romans.

3 — — — — — — — — —

A regiment of 1000 soldiers lived in this fort on Hadrian's Wall.

4 — — — — — — — —

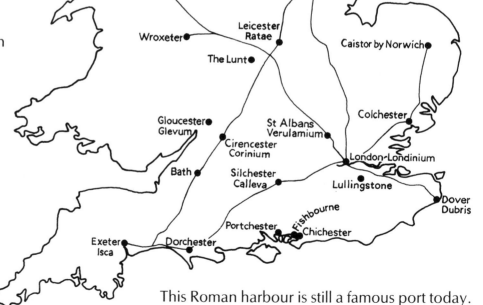

This Roman harbour is still a famous port today.

5 — — — — —

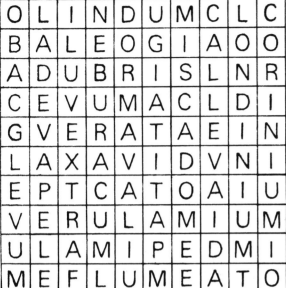

O	L	I	N	D	U	M	C	L	C
B	A	L	E	O	G	I	A	O	O
A	D	U	B	R	I	S	L	N	R
C	E	V	U	M	A	C	L	D	I
G	V	E	R	A	T	A	E	I	N
L	A	X	A	V	I	D	V	N	I
E	P	T	C	A	T	O	A	I	U
V	E	R	U	L	A	M	I	U	M
U	L	A	M	I	P	E	D	M	I
M	E	F	L	U	M	E	A	T	O

There are 11 Roman town names written in Latin hidden in this WORDSQUARE. See how many you can spot. The map will help you.

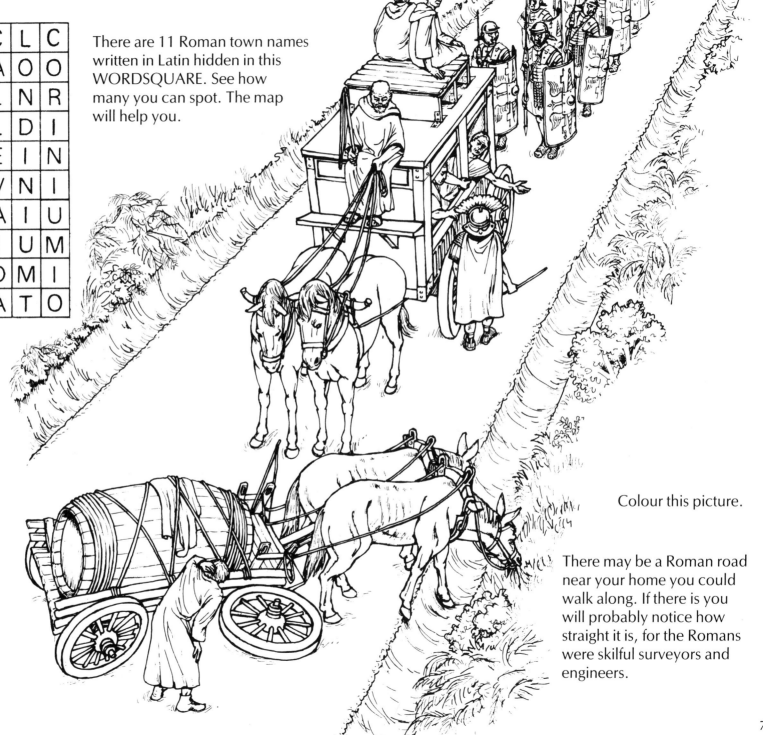

Good roads were very important to the Romans. They made it possible for officials, soldiers and traders to travel quickly to most parts of the province. However hold-ups like this must have been common when farmers took their produce to market. Gaius and his military escort are on the way from Dover to Chester (250 miles).

Soldiers were trained to march 25 miles a day. How long do you think it would take to get there?

Colour this picture.

There may be a Roman road near your home you could walk along. If there is you will probably notice how straight it is, for the Romans were skilful surveyors and engineers.

Money

denarius; silver

sestertius; made of
yellow metal like
a £1 coin

as; copper
like a 2p piece

(coins shown are actual size)

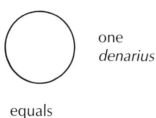

one
denarius

equals

four
sestertii

equal

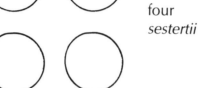

sixteen
asses

A legionary soldier earned about 300 *denarii* a year and although the army kept more than half of this for food, equipment and savings, legionaries were still richer than most ordinary people.

Soldiers were paid in silver *denarii* or gold coins called *aurei*. The *aureus* was the same size as a *denarius*, but much more valuable. It was worth 25 *denarii*, or 100 *sestertii*, or 400 *asses*.

Design your own coin in the space below. Use yourself or your best friend as a model. Don't forget to write your name and birthday round the edge.

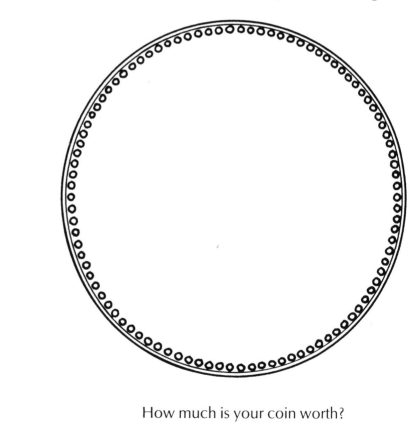

How much is your coin worth?

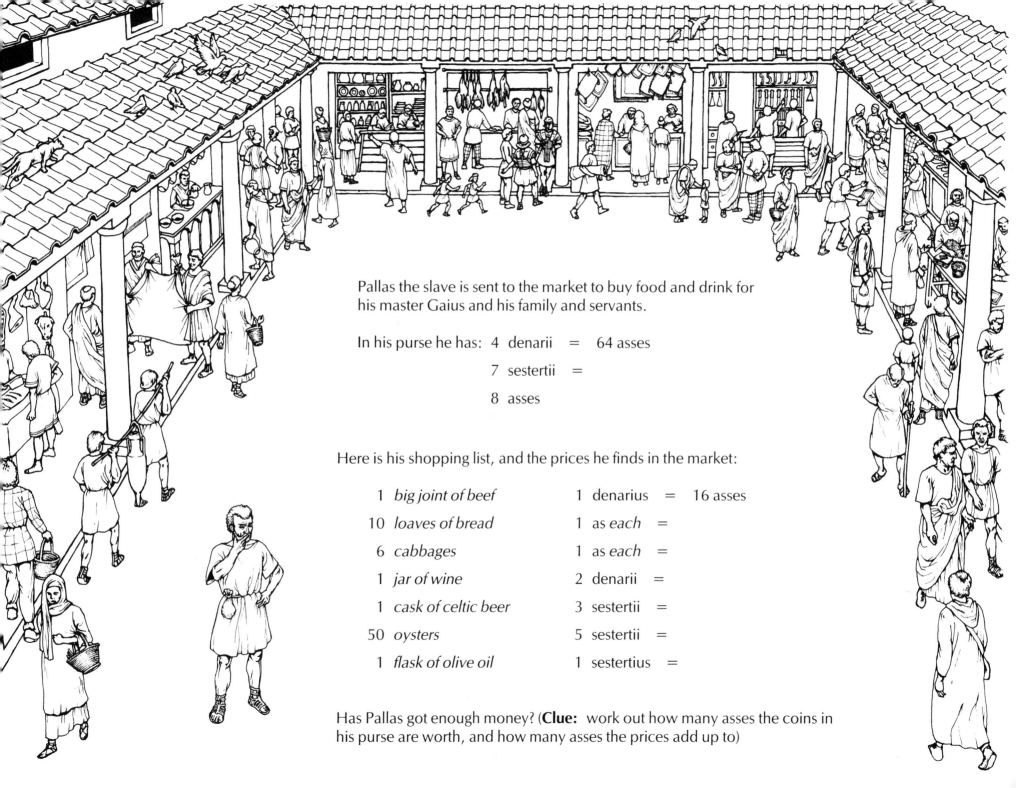

Pallas the slave is sent to the market to buy food and drink for his master Gaius and his family and servants.

In his purse he has: 4 denarii = 64 asses

7 sestertii =

8 asses

Here is his shopping list, and the prices he finds in the market:

1	*big joint of beef*	1 denarius =	16 asses
10	*loaves of bread*	1 as *each* =	
6	*cabbages*	1 as *each* =	
1	*jar of wine*	2 denarii =	
1	*cask of celtic beer*	3 sestertii =	
50	*oysters*	5 sestertii =	
1	*flask of olive oil*	1 sestertius =	

Has Pallas got enough money? (**Clue:** work out how many asses the coins in his purse are worth, and how many asses the prices add up to)

Gods and goddesses

Mercury   **Mars**   **Venus**   **Minerva**   **Jupiter**

We recognise some gods in statues and carvings from the things they wore or had with them. Follow the strings to name five of the most important Roman gods shown here

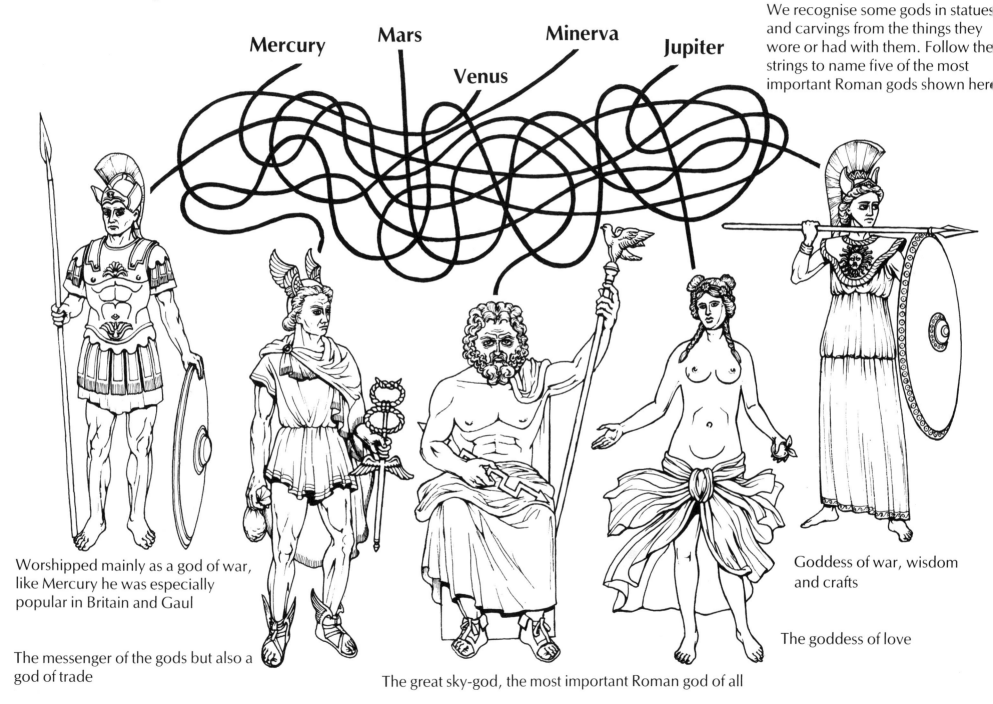

Worshipped mainly as a god of war, like Mercury he was especially popular in Britain and Gaul

The messenger of the gods but also a god of trade

The great sky-god, the most important Roman god of all

Goddess of war, wisdom and crafts

The goddess of love

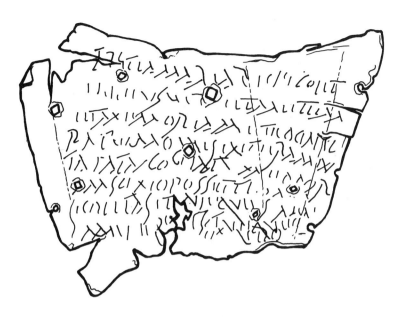

The people of the Roman Empire worshipped many different gods, both Roman and native ones. Sometimes a Roman god or goddess was joined with a local one, like Sulis–Minerva. You can see the remains of her temple at Bath.

Mithras was a Persian god of light whose followers performed mysterious ceremonies and had to undergo tests of bravery and endurance. Many were soldiers who were used to strict discipline. Temples of Mithras were small and often built partly underground. You can see the remains of one Temple of Mithras near Queen Victoria Street in London.

Prayers and offerings were regularly made to the gods in the hope of being rewarded with a healthy and happy life. Quite often people asked a god to help them get back something that had been stolen or to punish someone they did not like. A message was scratched on a piece of lead called a 'curse' or *defixio*.

The one above, found in London, says: 'I curse Tretia Maria and her life and mind and memory and liver and lungs mixed up together, and her words, thoughts and memory; thus may she be unable to speak what things are concealed, nor be able . . . nor . . .'

Here is a picture of a Romano–Celtic temple to colour in. It might have been built of stone or wood or a mixture of the two. Gaius might have taken some coins or food there as an offering. What would you take?

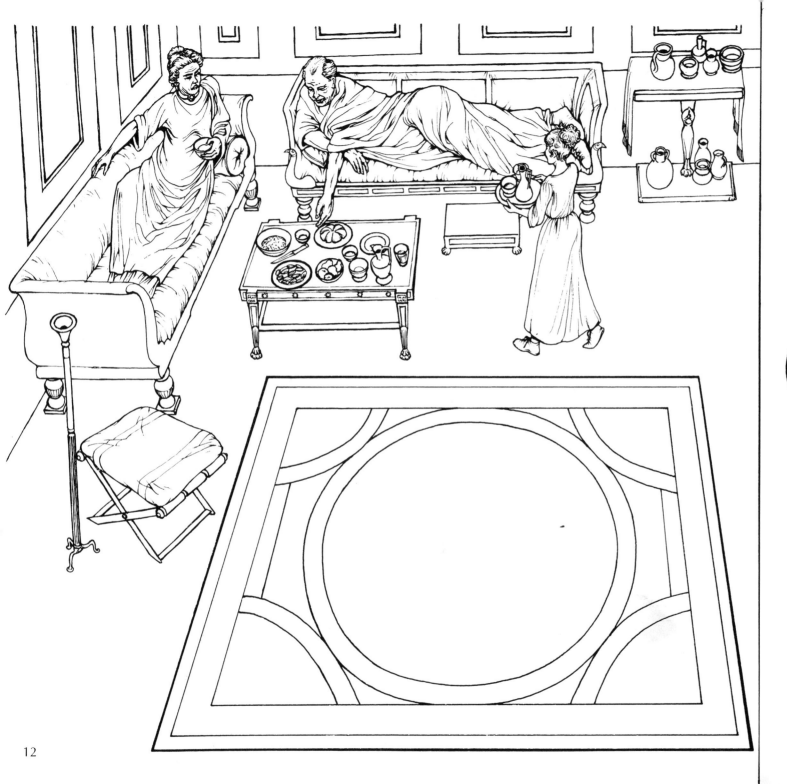

Mosaics

Many rich Romans had mosaics in their houses and villas. You can see some fine ones at Fishbourne.

Here are some of the patterns they used to decorate them.

Sometimes an animal or a god would be shown in the middle.

Finish the mosaic shown here and colour the whole picture. You could also make your own mosaic with pieces of coloured paper.

Hunting

This was a popular pastime as many wild animals lived in the forests including stags, wolves and bears. Gaius is hunting a wild boar. Which trail should he follow?

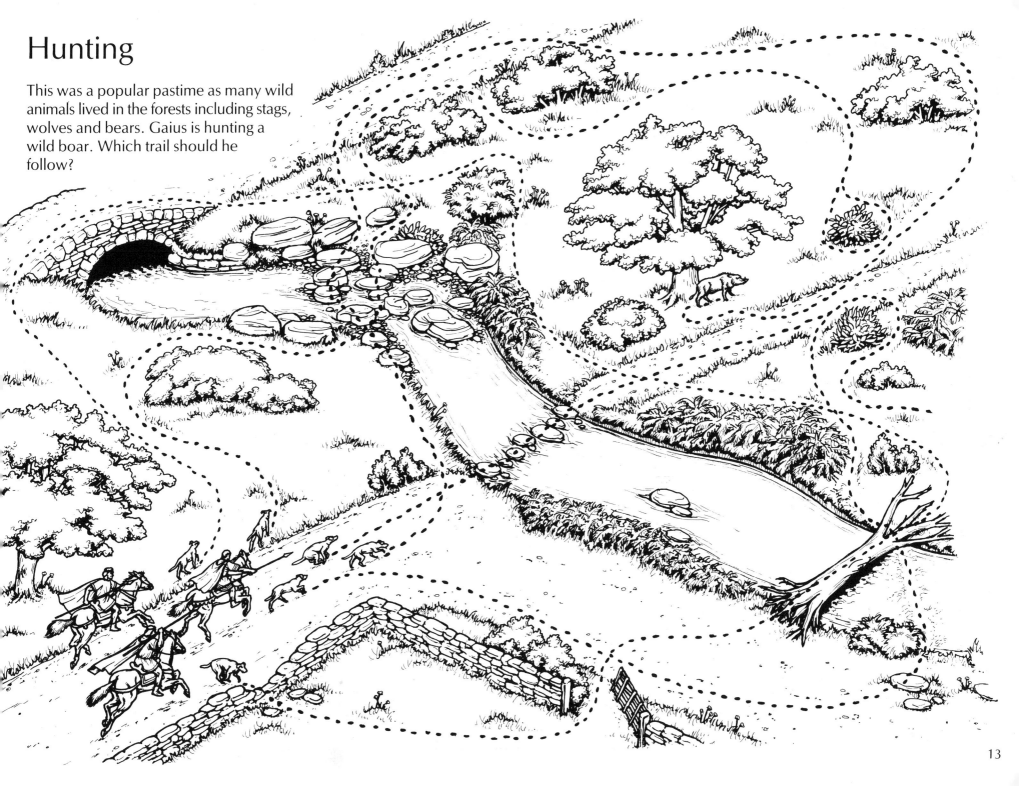

A ....
B ....
C ....
D ....

Soon after Gaius takes command of his legion trouble breaks out in the north of England. He sends a mixed force of cavalry and infantry to fight the enemy. Because the Romans are well-armed and have been carefully trained they are soon victorious.

After the battle the legionary blacksmith repairs the broken weapons and armour. Here a centurion (B), a standard bearer (C) and two other soldiers (A, D) are waiting to collect their equipment.

Look closely at the picture opposite. Identify these different soldiers and decide who owns what. Write in the answers (check them on p.16) and colour in the pictures.

Writing

In 1973 an exciting discovery was made at the fort of Vindolanda near Hadrian's Wall. Over 200 Roman writing tablets were found. They were made of very thin slices of wood which had been preserved by the waterlogged ground. Letters, food lists and other accounts had been written on them using pen and ink.

One tablet is part of a private letter to a soldier. It says:

'I have sent you . . . socks from Sattua, two pairs of sandals and two pairs of underpants . . .'

Some of the letters were written at the time when the Roman army started building Hadrian's Wall, in AD122.

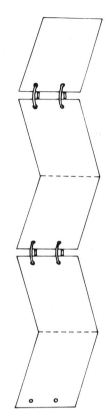

The emperor Hadrian had decided that a wall was needed to protect the civilised Roman province of Britannia from the warlike tribes of northern England and Scotland.

Imagine you are a soldier living at Vindolanda. Write a letter to a friend describing what it is like in your fort and working on the wall. Perhaps you could ask your friend to send some things that you cannot buy at Vindolanda. You could make a folding letter of cardboard like the wooden tablets.

If you want to know more about the Romans try to visit some of the sites shown on the map on page 6 and go to your local museum. You could also look at *The Time Traveller book of Rome and Romans* (Usborne) and Mike Corbishley's *The Romans,* History as Evidence series (Kingfisher).

English Heritage, which looks after nearly 400 of the most important monuments in England, has a special membership scheme for children called *Keep.* If you are interested, write for more information to English Heritage, PO Box 43, Ruislip, Middlesex HA4 0XW.

The *Young Archaeologists Club* is a national club for children aged 9 and over. The club offers a variety of archaeological activities, a magazine four times a year and special holidays. If you would like more details, write to Dr Kate Pretty, New Hall, Cambridge CB3 0DF.

Answers for

page 2   1 Nero; 2 Trajan; 3 Marcus Aurelius; 4 Hadrian

page 4   TV aerial; clock; tractor; zebra crossing; spectacles; bicycle; cassette player; vacuum flask

page 6   1 York; 2 Bath; 3 Fishbourne; 4 Housesteads; 5 Dover

page 15   A shield and spear; B shin guards; C standard; D sword and armour

Devised by Ralph Jackson, Simon James and Emma Mye

Drawings by William Webb

© 1986 The Trustees of the British Museum
Published by British Museum Press
a division of The British Museum Company Ltd
46 Bloomsbury Street, London WC1B 3QQ
11th impression 1997

ISBN 0–7141–1282–8

Printed in Great Britain by
St Edmundsbury Press Ltd, Bury St Edmunds, Suffolk